■ SCHOLASTIC
News
Nonfiction Readers

A Bear Cub Grows Up

by
Pam Zollman

Children's Press®
A Division of Scholastic Inc.
New York Toronto London Auckland Sydney
Mexico City New Delhi Hong Kong
Danbury, Connecticut

These content vocabulary word builders
are for grades 1-2.

Consultant: Dr. Lynn Rogers
Principal Biologist, Wildlife Research Institute

Curriculum Specialist: Linda Bullock

Special thanks to the Kansas City Zoo

Photo Credits:

Photographs © 2005: Animals Animals/Norbert Rosing: 5 top right, 8; Corbis Images: 23 top left (Robert Pickett), 5 bottom left, 9 (Scott T. Smith); Dembinsky Photo Assoc.: cover center inset (Claudia Adams), cover right inset, 20 top right, 21 top left (Dominique Braud), cover background, back cover, 20 bottom right, 21 top right (Bill Lea), 23 bottom left (Skip Moody); Lynn & Donna Rogers: 4 bottom left, 5 bottom right, 16, 17, 21 bottom left, 21 center right; Minden Pictures: 4 top, 11 (Jim Brandenburg), 15 (Matthias Breiter), 2, 4 bottom right, 7 (Yva Momatiuk/John Eastcott); Photo Researchers, NY: 5 top left, 13 (Tom Bledsoe), 1, 19 (Jeff Lepore), 23 top right (Steve & Dave Maslowski), cover left inset, 20 center right (Len Rue Jr.); Visuals Unlimited: 20 top left (Bill Banaszewski), 23 bottom right (Joe McDonald).

Book Design: Simonsays Design!

Library of Congress Cataloging-in-Publication Data

Zollman, Pam.
  A bear cub grows up / by Pam Zollman.
     p. cm. – (Scholastic news nonfiction readers)
  Includes bibliographical references (p.   ) and index.
  ISBN 0-516-24943-6 (lib. bdg.)
  1. Bear cubs–Juvenile literature. 2. Bears–Juvenile literature. I. Title.
     II. Series.
QL737.C27Z65 2005
599.78'139–dc22

                                                2005003291

1 2 3 4 5 6 7 8 9 10 R 14 13 12 11 10 09 08 07 06 05

CONTENTS

Word Hunt 4-5

Bear Cubs! 6-7

Cubs Nurse 8-9

Cubs Climb 10-11

Cubs Find Food 12-15

Cubs Hibernate 16-17

Cubs Grow 18-19

Timeline:
  A Bear Cub Grows Up! 20-21

Your New Words 22

What Else Hibernates? 23

Index 24

Find Out More 24

Meet the Author 24

WORD HUNT

Look for these words as you read. They will be in **bold**.

climb
(klime)

hibernate
(**hye**-bur-nate)

mammal
(**mam**-uhl)

4

cub
(kuhb)

den
(den)

nurse
(nurs)

rake
(rayk)

Bear Cubs!

A bear is a **mammal**.

Mammals have hair and give birth to babies.

A baby bear is called a **cub.**

Do you know when a bear cub is born?

bear cubs

A mother bear makes a **den** in the winter.

One or more cubs are born in the den.

The mother bear **nurses** her babies.

She keeps them warm, too.

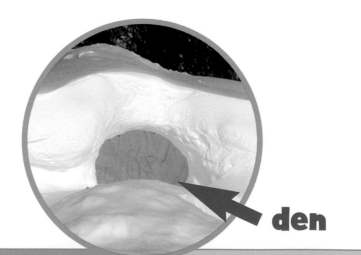

den

These bear cubs are nursing.
They are feeding on their mother's milk.

9

Now it is spring!

The bears go outside.

The cubs like to run and **climb** trees.

They can climb very high.

What are these
cubs doing?

They are watching
their mother.

She teaches them how
to find food.

They copy everything
she does.

Mother bear teaches her cubs how to catch fish.

13

Cubs learn what is good to eat.

They like nuts and fruits.

Fish and bugs taste good, too.

Cubs eat a lot and get fat.

This cub is eating a fish. Yum!

Now it is fall. It is time to get ready for winter.

The cubs help their mother **rake** leaves for beds.

Winter comes.

Mother bear and her cubs **hibernate**, or sleep.

hibernate

These cubs are raking leaves to make a bed.

Spring comes again.

The bears come outside.

Most bear cubs will grow up by fall.

Soon, each bear will start a new family.

A BEAR CUB GROWS UP!

1 ....

It is fall. Mother bear finds a den to hibernate. She will give birth to cubs in the winter.

2 ....

Mother bear and her cubs wake up in the spring.

3 ....

Cubs learn what to eat and how to hunt in the summer.

7 Now it is summer.
This cub is a fully-grown-bear now.

6 It is spring again. The cubs are almost grown-up. They will leave their mother soon.

5 Mother bear and her cubs hibernate during the winter.

4 It is time to get ready for winter. The cubs rake leaves into a den.

YOUR NEW WORDS

climb (klime) bears climb, or go up, trees

cub (kuhb) animals like baby lions,
    wolves, and bears are cubs

den (den) a cave or hollow tree where
    bears sleep during the winter

hibernate (hye-bur-nate) to sleep through
    the winter

mammal (mam-uhl) a warm-blooded
    animal that nurses its babies
    and is covered with hair

nurse (nurs) to feed a baby its
    mother's milk

rake (rayk) bears rake, or collect, leaves
    to make beds

WHAT ELSE HIBERNATES?

A ladybug!

A skunk!

A toad!

A woodchuck!

23

INDEX

birth, 8
bugs, 14

climbing, 10
cubs, 5, 6, 8, 10, 12, 14,
    16, 18

dens, 5, 8

eating, 14

fish, 14

food, 12, 14
fruits, 14

hair, 6
hibernation, 4, 16

leaves, 16

mammals, 4, 6
mothers, 8, 12, 16

nursing, 5, 8

nuts, 14

raking, 5, 16
running, 10

spring, 10, 18

winter, 8, 16

FIND OUT MORE

Book:

Watch Me Grow: Bear, by Lisa Magloff (DK Publishing, 2003)

Website:

http://www.enchantedlearning.com/subjects/mammals/bear/

MEET THE AUTHOR:

Pam Zollman is the award-winning author of short stories, articles, and books for kids. She is the author of *North Dakota* (Scholastic/Children's Press) and the other Life Cycle books in this series. She lives in rural Pennsylvania where she has seen bears much closer than she would like.